The
AFFLICTED
GIRLS

"Ophelia" (c.1851) by John Everett Millais (1829-1896)

Winner of the
Vernice Quebodeaux "Pathways" Poetry Prize for Women

THE AFFLICTED GIRLS

Cathleen Calbert

FIRST EDITION

Little Red Tree Publishing, LLC,
North Platte, Nebraska, 69101

Copyright © 2016 Cathleen Calbert

All rights are reserved under International and Pan-American Copyright Conventions. Except for brief passages quoted in a newspaper, magazine, radio or television review, no part of this book may be reproduced in any form or by any means, electronic or mechanical, including photocopying and recording, or by any information storage and retrieval system, without permission in writing from the publisher.

Layout and Cover Design: Michael Linnard
Text in Minion Pro, Trajan Pro and Arial.

First Edition, 2016 manufactured in USA
1 2 3 4 5 6 7 8 9 10 LSI 20 19 18 17 16

All previous publication credits of a number of poems in this collection are listed at the back of this book [page 99].

Front cover painting is a "Study for Ophelia" (1852) by John Everett Millais (1829-1896).

Photograph of Cathleen Calbert on back cover and page 107 by Jess Duckett.

Paintings reproduced on pages i, 1, 89, 97, and 101, are separately attributed

Library of Congress Cataloging-in-Publication Data

Calbert, Cathleen
　The Afflicted Girls / Cathleen Calbert. -- 1st ed.
　　p. cm.
　Includes index
　ISBN 978-1-935656-44-9 (pbk. : alk. paper)
　I. Title. II. Index.
　PS3612.A58565S77 2015
　811'.6--dc23

Little Red Tree Publishing LLC
509 W 3rd Street,
North Platte, Nebraska 69101
www.littleredtree.com

Contents

Author's Note	xiii
First Wife	3
Assumption	4
Sainted Ladies of the Middle Ages	6
Heretic	8
The Afflicted Girls	10
The Wild Girl of Champagne	12
Pirating	13
Genius	16
At Chawton Cottage	18
The Lambs	20
"The Misses Bronte's Establishment for The Board and Education of a Limited Number of Young Ladies"	21
Motherhood	24
Dear Miss Dickinson,	26
A Case of Nerves	28
Stunner	29
Effie Ruskin, 1849	33
Séance	35
Nightingale	36
Wandering Womb	38
Augustine, Photographed at the Salpêtrière	41
Talking Cure	42
Lizzie Borden Bed and Breakfast Museum	43
Mata Hari	45
Queen Alice	47
Teacher	49
Flapper	51
Blood in London	52
New Yorker	55

La Gran Ocultadora	56
Fairy Tale	57
Confession to the Moon	60
Suicide's Daughter	62
Jayne Mansfield and Isadora Duncan	64
à la mode	65
The Breast Monologues	67
Miss Bishop Has Left the Building	69
Florida	71
Molly Finn, Taken by the Sea	75
Ocean State	77
Teen Vamp	79
Hitherto Undisclosed Categories of Unfortunate Demise	82
Mash Up: Rush Meets Feral Pigs in the Champlain Valley	84
Skin	86
The Princess Bride	87
Notes	91
Previous Publishing Credits	99
Index: titles and first lines	103
About the Author	106

For
Christopher Mayo
(Reader, I married him)

&

Remembering
Barbara Mortimer
(The kindest one of all)

ACKNOWLEDGMENTS

The author gratefully thanks:

Michael Linnard for choosing this collection as the winner of the Vernice Quebodeaux "Pathways" Poetry Prize for Women and thus providing a home to the *Afflicted Girls*, some of whom, like Heathcliff's ghostly Cathy, have been hoping to be let in for a while.

All the editors of the publications, listed at the back of the book, for first publishing a number of the poems, sometimes in different versions and/or under different titles.

Rhode Island College for providing the time needed to write the poems.

My teachers, friends, and students for infusing a spark of being into the poems and helping to bring "my girls" to life.

Author's Note

A number of years ago, I wrote a few dramatic monologues; then, as happens, I wrote a few more. Then a few more . . .

I wandered around the library at Macalester College, dragging home books through the snow. I wandered around Salem, gathering up pamphlets about those infamous trials. I wandered around soggy London, then tramped through the English countryside and tiptoed through homes of my literary heroes. I gazed at Millais' painting of Ophelia, thinking of the strange truths uttered by Hamlet's madwoman and of Lizzie Siddal, Dante Gabriel Rossetti's wife, sadly but beautifully posing as her.

I felt released and renewed poetically as I pieced together portraits of various women, with no other agenda except my own wayward interests. It was nice to think about others' lives and write in response to them. However, I don't mean to claim that everything I have written regarding historical personages is "true." Despite the nerdy research, this collection isn't meant to be a work of scholarship, and I invoke "poetic license."

Richard Howard, my former teacher and a famous donner of poetic masks, once wrote, "I'll tell my state as though 'twere none of mine." Such is the nature of dramatic monologues, of course. In Adrienne Rich's lovely epistolary poem "Paula Becker to Clara Westhoff," the voices of the turn-of-the-century artist Paula Becker and Rich herself are intermingled, entwined. And I know my own less spectacular history shadows my subjects in this collection.

Finally, I might add that in the second decade of the 21st century, I see in fiction and film many strong young women: brave, noble, kind, true. They surely will affect the next generation for the better, and I'm glad for that. Yet I remain, perversely perhaps, attracted to afflicted girls: bright but troubled, beleaguered and embittered, funny but dangerous, righteous and wrong.

Such is the nature of poems and poets, I suppose: to enjoy a perpetual play of opposites.

Cathleen Calbert
Pacific Grove, California

"Ophelia" (c.1851) by John Everett Millais (1829-1896)

FIRST WIFE

Marriage was new for both of us.
        All that came easily was bickering.

I gave up on him and flew into the wind,
        past smoking lava hills, past fresh valleys,

landing alone on the shore, where I wove
        shells and kelp into the earliest necklaces,

then sported with silken sea creatures,
        loving their soft tongues and webbed toes.

The man complained, and God listened.
        He sent three messengers to warn me:

I must return or He would take away
        one hundred of my sons by morning,

but they had become grains of sand
        and the fine lace of foam on my skin.

The story goes that I seek vengeance,
        returning in a fury from the Red Sea.

My kiss is death, yet my words are
        wine, my hands warm as fire,

my dress iridescent, my hair a mess
        of colors strangling one another.

Like a cat, I suck out men's breaths
        as they sleep beside their wives

wearing amulets with my likeness
        bound in fetters, wings limp, as if

I were a captured bird when I was
        the first, come from no one's rib.

ASSUMPTION

Little is known of her earthly existence
    except that a son treated her rudely,
        she wasn't included in any doings
            of the Apostles, didn't turn into a pillar
of the Church, said little, and wrote nothing,
    yet she alone achieved ascension to heaven
        without suffering the awful process
            of putrefaction, that ooze into dust
(if not officially floating up until 1950).
    Only she can be with Christ bodily;
        only they can dance the dance of flesh.
            Early on, at the Council of Chalcedon,
she did acquire the title "Aeiparthenos."
    Achrantos. Aminatos. Theotokos.
        Virgo intacta, in partu, postpartum.
            Not impregnated by human or sacred seed,
she conceived, in a manner of speaking,
    via the ear, like a medieval weasel,
        through the word of the Holy Spirit.
            Oxymoronic virgin/mother of Jesus
and the rest of us, she wasn't hot enough
    to be the lover of God the Father,
        just our heavy-hearted *Mater Dolorosa,*
            lachrymose half of the Pietà,
but the wonder of this pure pregnancy,
    o clemens, o pia, o dulcis Maria,
        made amends for that sneaky Eve,
            who brought down the curtain
and a curse on our heads. In return,
    Mary deserved a worship of her own:
        hyperdulia, Valley-speak for extreme veneration,
            not the garden-variety given to saints
(although never awarded "adoration,"
    which can be bestowed on God alone;
        our gods are not women).
            In Renaissance paintings, she moved

center stage, a commanding presence,
    stars overhead, crescent at her feet,
        her son's buddies in dumb awe,
            hands pressed to their lesser chests
as they beheld the Halo of Gold,
    Lily Among Thorns, Rose of Jericho,
        whose aroma was ambrosial,
            breath asphodel and storax,
breasts as fragrant as cloves, womb
    a spring shut up, fountain frozen.
        With no gravesite or shrine, she still drifts
            freely, all the universe a possibility
for the Immaculate Conception
    though we have struggled to hold on
        to what bits of her we can:
            nail pairings in a purse at Poitou,
hair, black to gold, collected from Rome
    to Assisi, fragments of clothing found
        as far away as San Salvador, her home
            transported to Slovenia and to Italy.

Sainted Ladies of the Middle Ages

I went for eleven days
nibbling only the flowers
from my father's lime tree
                                              For a fortnight,
                                              I swallowed fallen petals
                                              of roses soaked in rain
                       For the Feast of Our Lady,
                       I lapped up a little milk
                       to satisfy my family
If friends put fish to my lips,
I drained the juice but left the flesh
                                              I lived on sips of wine
                                              though I wished it
                                              were seawater
                     I took no eggs or meat
I choked down moldy bread
                                              I mixed ash in my mead
                     I stirred in dirt
I threw in small stones
                                              I added scabs and lice
                     I licked the dust in misery
I sucked pus from the dying
                                              I stopped perspiring
                   I stopped menstruating
I stopped eliminating
                                            I bled from my nose
                   I bled from my hands
I bled from my feet
                                          I shed bits of skin and teeth,
                                          which I gave to those in need
                   The aroma that rose
                   from my body caused
                   one of my confessors
                   to confess to me
My bathwater

    cooled the fever
    of our priest

                                             My breasts swelled with oil
                                             and made a helpful salve
                                             for the sores of my sisters
                       My breasts filled with enough milk
                       to nurse the whole village
I pressed our Lord to my chest,
blessed to feed
the Lamb of God

                                             A silver chalice
                                              replenished my love
                    The Host was honeycomb
                    upon my tongue
This is His body,
This is His blood

HERETIC

She donned a man's doublet and tunic,
    then left home without permission,

drawn on by an angel, not seen in visions
    but with *the eyes of her body.*

The Maid was free from ladies' maladies,
    yet Ménière's disease did the trick,

lighting and chiming her way into history:
    a rare woman leads men to their deaths.

When an arrow pierced one shoulder
    on her bloody march as *chef de guerre,*

she let her women dress it with olive oil
    before driving out the camp followers

with warning blows from the flat of a sword
    to keep her troops as clean as the Lord's.

Thrown in a tower, she leapt. Her captors
    picked up the broken marionette,

shaved her head as a penitent and dressed
    their prisoner in women's clothing.

Soldier or symbol? Virgin or wanton?
    Leader or mascot? Man or woman?

Pressed by their questions, she wept bitterly.
    I guess this was her Gethsemane.

She didn't want to burn. She didn't want
    a consummation of skin and bones.

Christ himself quailed as he saw his ending,
> but I hear a girl, not a saint, crying,

Rouen, Rouen, am I to die here?
> Youth believes most in its immortality.

The Afflicted Girls

Some said it was Unnatural
        Rebellion against God and Man
sprung from a Stubbornness
        of Mind or unmaidenly Pride,

but this Affliction had no Mortal
        Cause and no human remedy,
the fault that of the Father of Lies,
        who improved our tongues

to speak of things we knew not of
        as we Christened the Minister
"Blackguard," "Damnable Rogue,"
        and "Whoremasterly Hellhound."

We cast aside his Bible, crying,
        "These are only goblin stories!
Why, the Prince of this World offers
        more than Sin and Misery!"

After we collapsed in his arms,
        we admitted the Tempter
of Souls had promised us Canaries
        or ribbons if we dined with him.

But he had enchanted the pudding,
        so we grew faint, almost Falling,
as he pressed us to add our X's
        to his Book, below the names

of Hades' Handmaidens, the fallen
        women who told us in dreams
to come dance with the Black Man,
        for someday we must marry.

Since we confessed our Bewitchment,
        we were called upon to Testify,
providing the Spectral Evidence
        of who let Demons enter them.

At the first Sentencing, one insisted,
        "I have no skill in Witchery."
Then she tried, "I will unwitch the girls,
        just let me speak," meaning *Lie*.

We looked to the truth of her body,
        hunting for the hidden teat.
It always is cold, the Devil's own;
        if pricked, a witch feels nothing.

Unwholesome Mother, she succored
        Night Creatures that suck blood
from lower lips and milk from ring fingers.
        We envisioned her Familiars:

one similar to a Cat with bat wings,
        another rather like a Monkey,
eyes in the back of its head gaping
        as it gulped her secret Elixir.

Unable to disclose the magic pap,
        we loosened our own clothing
to reveal blisters from the Hell-Fire
        this Night-Flier had fed in us.

They seized the Scold, Troublemaker,
        Quarrelsome Shrew, and hanged her
at our word as if we were men or queens.
        We swore before the Congregation

that we would become Good Wives,
        not discontent with our condition,
and we would live Righteous Lives,
        our thoughts turned up to Heaven.

The Wild Girl of Champagne

Rags hung from the blackened body,
But "la sauvage" was civilized enough
To carry a club and, in one blow, dispose
Of the bulldog that clung to her ankle
As she snatched apples in an orchard.

Monsieur d'Epinay, the village nobleman,
Said to capture the girl, save her, bring her
Under the King's and God's dominion,
So a townswoman tempted her down
To earth with eels and a pail of water.

She thrilled crowds with her howls,
Manly love of meat, and lapping up drink
Like a dog; however, before long, her
Fondness for raw frogs was discouraged,
And washing with lye whitened her skin.

Christened Marie Angélique Le Blanc,
She got shipped off to a convent in Paris,
Then grew boring, no longer a curiosity
Like the chimpanzee that wowed London,
Dwarf Patagonian, or shocking Hottentot.

When her benefactor died, the Sisters sent
Marie packing, yet she still believed God
Had not transformed Animal to Christian
Just to abandon His creation and the world
Would not forget her, but, of course, it did.

Pirating

I was a boy before I became a woman. My father hid his bastard
daughter in the guise of a sister's son. I skipped rocks far across

the water my steps longer than any girl's. As soon as I slipped
on a dress I met a boy who belonged to the sea who wasn't

worth a groat so said my father. He would give us nothing
from his rows of tobacco. I left the plantation in flames prepared

for the life of a seawife honest if rough. I was to sew up holes
in the lads' jackets knot the line wash down the deck. Except

we were boarded by self proclaimed kings of the sea and given
our choice keelhauling or putting in with them. While my man

mended sail the captain all in calico hiked up my skirt his hand
over my mouth. Would I have called out? As my father took his

wife's maid so Captain Jack took me. One cannot call that seduction
but once done there was a kind of love as harsh as the sun.

Our lives were not easy scurvy the bloody flux and the men
like as not to shoot themselves or blow us up drunk on rum

that ran as freely as ditch-water. When we could we plundered
brigantines laden with sugar bound for Madagascar and Mozambique.

We helped ourselves to citrons tamarinds black bananas honey
and coconuts matelote and mangoes sweeter than perfume.

On islands smaller than my father's farm I went turtling (the flesh
made a fine stew). I picked up a spider monkey which I wore

on one shoulder like a lady's lopsided wig. I saw the southern lights
seabirds as big as angels and as fierce. In Jamaica Jack bought

fair winds from a wind seller. He tried to buy me outright from
Mr. Bonny   but the magistrate   said that   I should be in chains

for turning libertine so we married ourselves by starlight then
rode the currents countryless. "Where do you hail from brothers?"

sailors cried. "From the sea!" we yelled as if self sprung like Venus
in her shell or Athena. I fought as a man far easier to load powder

or stuff a cutlass in breeches and a tar's blouson but the crew knew
me to be a woman as well. I was to foretell all storms and keep

devilfish from bleeding their toes or serpents from coiling themselves
around the anchor. Oh those boys were   a superstitious lot. Jellies

seemed   sunken virgins   to them   and giant polyps bore the faces
of lost mothers. Scylla   himself lifted   his six mouths   into the spray

and called them   to a watery grave.   When I bled they begged me
to lie   unclothed   under   the night sky so the currents   would follow

my bent and my body would frighten the behemoths that breathed
whirl winds. I indulged them more seawitch   than seaman then.

Yet when   we did battle   I demanded   that   each hand   fight
like a man or die like a dog. "Join or drown" we told   the crew

of a schooner   among them   a pretty boy   his face   as smooth
as a girl's. I took him   below and loosened my clothes   to show

I was not   what I seemed   my bosom   as soft   as his cheeks.
He undressed   and disclosed   breasts   larger than my own.

Sister to sister we lay together.   Above deck we gave no quarter
the last two left standing under the black flag. "A hell of our making"

declared   the judge. "Hang the dogs. Have mercy on their souls."
All swung. Captain Jack   they strung up on the bluffs of Kingston.

Mary and I pled our bellies. The seeds of men had taken root. No
steps and string for us until we were relieved of our burdens.

I held my girl in the damp gaol cell. I felt her heat rise to the skies
rise to heaven. Alone then I obliged Society with an orphan.

But someone my father? intervened enough bullion and I was free
to leave with a bastard of my own to raise. Damn his eyes. He can

set a place for me and mine all the days of his life if he
likes. I still walk on water. My daughter makes a fine first mate.

Together we have rounded Cape Horn the Cape of Good
Hope and gone on to uncharted waters where live the famed

fish tailed maids whose hair is as green as seafire. After sunset
their skin looks like that of dead men their eyes unholy emeralds.

Even I count them unlucky then but at dawn they bathe on rocks
and comb their seaweed tresses as they gaze into mirrors

encrusted with starfish and abalone at a past of endless waves
living in a way backwards as is their wont since they worship

the moon not the sun. They shall summon two sailors neither men
nor women to a feast under the sea whenever we tire of roving.

GENIUS

Tucked away at Grasmere, he spooled out
the cuckoo poem and the one about the idiot

as you transplanted snowdrops, then tried
to cover a little German and a little Chaucer

before tending to the batter pudding, a surprise
for William, from whom you asked nothing

but genius, gratified to have seen your eyes
in his verse and to serve as his memory,

as his boon companion on hillside rambles,
though he often paid no attention to things,

once confusing his sister with the scenery,
taking a sheep for you, and you for a sheep.

Yet you waxed romantic over his apple core.
Love like this is hard to swallow these days,

less so when you write of resting in the heather,
lying separately, listening to each other breathe;

such lonely togetherness must have been bliss,
your spot of time, a moment of timelessness.

Unfortunately, eternity on earth is fleeting.
At least he said goodbye to you in private.

You released the ring you wore: a blessing,
a divorce. Unwilling to come to the wedding,

you welcomed home your new sister, Mary,
whose children you'd tend until giving way

to "mental and physical collapse," the usual
formula of womanly surrender and victory:

no more housekeeping or heartfelt journeys
to visit the country folk you wrote of in diary

but only a poet could transform into poetry,
a gift the gods bestowed on your brother alone.

Yet in the end you felt he'd failed as well
and huddled by the fire even in springtime

when the northern climate lost a bit of its bite.
In 1802, you wrote on Christmas morning,

"I am 31 years of age.—It is a dull frosty day."
Eventually, the frost would come to stay.

AT CHAWTON COTTAGE

My hair blowzy with the breeze and humidity, my walking shoes
      thoroughly muddy from a morning tramp through Exmoor

among the paradoxically wild Shetland ponies, I am pleased
      to see that my red leather jacket is holding up admirably

(I'm a bright blotch against any landscape I stand in front of)
      as the guide directs me, with kind anxiety, to "Jane's things":

a pizza-pie-sized writing table and the door that (reportedly)
      creaked a warning. Lacking the distinction of being the spot

where the author breathed her last, this is, at least, where she took
      to dying, which she'd soon accomplish, at precisely my age,

an age that struck me, when I was young, as no longer being young.
      How deeply and superficially this thought saddens me.

Perhaps I already am carrying my own kernel of disease.
      Perhaps I will simply continue disintegrating. Either way,

I shouldn't be running madly after ridiculously little ponies.
      I should be chaperoning a dance, nubile nymphs gliding past,

young men stopping by to mop their brows and ask me how
      they might best approach their lithe Lynette or distant Cindy.

A carload of children is spilling out to the street. What a droll party!
      Their wordy T-shirts and candy-shining faces tire me instantly.

The mother, poor creature, is carrying another and bears the burden
      inelegantly, listing to either side as bears dance across her chest.

She must be in her twenties. Despite the middle-aged rotundity,
      her skin is peachy, and inside her body dwells life, not death.

There it is again. "Death. Death. Death. Death. Death." So Uncle Walt
    once wrote except I believe he meant to be happily incantatory,

not just obsessed, as I seem bent on becoming. And why should I be?
    After all, I'm still among the living. Perhaps it will be satisfying

to sit by the fire drinking wine in the evening with my husband
    or (if he leaves me for a younger woman) another companion,

a sensible friend or devoted sister, to pass on bits of amusing news,
    our tendencies towards irony balanced by a growing generosity.

I hold the door for the pitiable thing though I'm thinking, she's seen
    a recent film version, she probably longs to happen upon

Mr. Darcy or Mr. Knightly. On cue, she tells me, "I love her movies."
    I waver on the precipice, lips curving into a cutting comment.

It would be easy, and I've grown mean, squirreled away in my studies,
    but I will embrace, not despise, life as it comes, for the world

is filled with sponge cakes, clotted cream, and tiny, wild ponies.
    I nod my assent. We are, I assure her, in complete agreement.

THE LAMBS

Well, she is gone, mad again, and dearest Charles—
    I will not condescend to call him "poor," as he loathes
        to hear himself pitied—awaits her return from Hoxton.

In her first bout of illness, the sole woman Will Hazlitt
    allowed as capable of reason struck their mother down,
        vowing she would understand her "better in heaven."

Heartbroken, Charles pledged that he would give up
    poetry, that he would burn everything. I warned him
        not to succumb to the temptation of self-destruction.

In return, he told me I should cultivate filial feelings.
    I had married rashly, out of passion for an ideology,
        not a woman, and remain devoted to my own demons,

yet my friend stays half in awe of me, afraid of losing
    his identity in mine and fearful that my wild wit might
        prompt Mary to "dance within an inch of the precipice."

I think they are best left alone, "a double singleness."
    Wedded in tragedy, he shall pine for his sister and only
        be at peace when she is fit, penning verses for children.

Indeed, he was wrong about writing. It is what saves us
    from despair, forestalling the final destitution of spirit
        that follows when the imagination will no longer flare.

"The Misses Brontë's Establishment for the Board and Education of a Limited Number of Young Ladies"

We've been trading with each other:
        Dr. Johnson for Rossetti, Shandy Hall

for the Brontës' Parsonage. I haven't
        driven any of the eight hundred miles

we've logged in England. I had wanted
        to try, but there's a fine line between

trying and killing two or more people
        instantly, so I've directed, often badly.

That's why he's speaking in sentences
        of two to three words, and I'm crying

when we hit Haworth proper, but I clutch
        his hand as I stumble up and down

ankle-breaking cobblestone streets,
        looking to him for balance, as always.

When I suggest that he carry me,
        he says, "I'll drag you if necessary."

He's not exactly kidding. I am afraid
        we've taken too long getting lost

and fighting, that the day has grown
        late, or maybe it only seems late

since we're able to pay and pore over
        glass cases of the sisters' things

(ink well, books, small hats and gloves).
        I decide I'm not feeling well

and need to rest in the cemetery,
        where it's easier to breathe,

the graves not a source of pestilence
        as they were in the nineteenth century.

Who am I to view their belongings?
        It seems like an invasion, a violation,

especially of Emily, who admired Byron
        as a "champion of unsocial man,"

who resisted losing her anonymity,
        who punched her dog in the eyes,

making him bleed, when she found him
        sleeping on the forbidden bed.

Charlotte was right. There's nothing
        romantic here: "if she demand beauty

to inspire her, she must bring it inborn."
        "The world within," right, Emily?

"Liberty" her "life's breath," among these
        scruffy, ugly hills. I can't see it,

but I haven't come in the spring
        when there are daffodils and bilberries

or been here in September when heather
        gives everything new meaning.

I guess we'd give the moors a try—
        we've seen women walking in twos

and threes, heads together, baguettes
        and bottled water in backpacks—

except we can't find parking, so we stroll
        along Main Street, poking into shops

with placards bearing their poor likenesses
        (Branwell wasn't much of an artist).

We find aromatherapy, love potions,
        and heather-scented heart pillows

as if *Wuthering Heights* were *Kama Sutra*
        "love" oil. I don't find it that amusing.

There's nothing here for me, so goodnight,
        ladies. Anne, God keep you safe.

Charlotte, thank you for Jane. Emily,
        you bully, you terror, what can I say?

Too proud to lie down for dying,
        you believed the bondage of this life

would end in an eternity of your choosing
        among the furze and the bracken.

As for us, we're off to the Lake Country
        to find the sublime. When we leave,

I hear girls whisper, "The Gondals are
        discovering the interior of Gaaldine."

Motherhood

"My dolls were Queens, not babies..."
Charlotte Perkins Gilman

"Let me speak the plain truth—
    my sufferings are very great—
        my nights indescribable":
Charlotte Brontë. A student titles her essay
    "The Last Day That I Came First."
        I go over a draft and encourage her,
yet the final version is a mess;
    pieced together, contradictory, it ends
        with a brief paean to mothering.
She tells me, "My husband couldn't believe
    I'd complain about our baby."
        De Beauvoir: "Childbearing,
at the moment, is real slavery."
    An aide taking my blood pressure asks,
        "How many children do you have?"
"We talked of poetry, and also of infanticide":
    Adrienne Rich. Charlotte Perkins Gilman:
        "Human motherhood is more
pathological than any other,
    morbid, defective, irregular, diseased."
        Plath: "Being born a woman
is my awful tragedy . . . .
    I deserve a year, two years,
        to live my own self into being."
"I don't get what Gilman's problem is.
    It's awesome to have children":
        a section of Honors Composition.
Two of them already are parents;
    the rest, as far as I can discern, are virgins.
        My brother's first wife: "Give it a try!"
Rachel: "Give me children, or else I die."
    Susan B. Anthony to Antoinette Brown:

    "Now Nettie, *not another baby.*"
A pal and fellow Ph.D.
  on her pregnancy: "Not all of us
    have ice water in our veins."
In class, a boy asks a girl,
  "Don't you want to have children?"
    They can't be old enough to drink legally.
"Ah, how I do repent me of the male faces
  I have washed, the mittens I have knit":
    Elizabeth Cady Stanton.
Susan Smith begging for someone
  to find her babies. "Nothing like a mom
    to make you feel better,"
one niece nudges a young cousin.
  Psychoanalyst Alice Balint: "The ideal
    mother has no interests of her own."
"I realize, with guilt, that I am a woman . . . .
  (How can you really know
    what I mean—you have never been
worn down by a nagging child?)":
  Sexton's journal for a male therapist.
    "Please tell me if I get obnoxious":
my best friend, pregnant at 41. Calamity
  Jane to her distant daughter, Janey:
    "I mind my own business but always
remember that is one thing
  the world hates is a woman
    who minds her own business."

Dear Miss Dickinson,

I wouldn't mind sleeping with Shelley or Keats
    if either of them were alive and well enough,
        but it's you that I want to grab hold of
            and make answer all my questions. Tell me,
                Beauty's kangaroo, Death's girlfriend,
                    from our perspective in the 21st century,
            how would you classify your problem?
        Agoraphobia? Social anxiety?
    New England eccentricity?
Higginson never fully believed
his lily-wielding, partially cracked acolyte
    even wrote poetry. How you drained him.
        "Without touching her, she drew from me."
            He only wanted to help you learn control,
                but his range was too narrow for a girl
                    who'd become the grande dame
                  of American letters, yours by the White Election,
            isn't that what you said? "Queen Recluse,"
        Samuel Bowles shouted up the stairs for you
    to cut out the nonsense and come down.
You obeyed. You laughed. You were witty.
    Obviously, you weren't always crazy.
        What I want to know is:
            Did you know what you were doing?
                Did you have trouble rhyming?
                    Were the dashes because you were lazy?
                Or were the verses really journal entries,
            valentines to a world that never wrote to you?
        If so, why not burn the neatly sewn parcels
    to better keep your Barefoot-Rank?
Surely you knew you were dying.
    "Little Cousins, Called back—Emily."
        This farewell note makes me want to cry.
            But I wish I knew why you wrote
                as you did. Were you thinking—

in gaps? A heap of broken images?
Kicking off modern poetry alone
in your room in the 19th century?
But how could that be?
366 poems in 1862? What did you do?
One a day plus an extra for good measure?
How could you write at that rate?
Didn't you ever masturbate?
I mean, you were a grown woman.
Did you or did you not die a virgin?
Were you a lesbian? In love
with Sister Sue or simply affectionate
in a way we can't understand
as anything other than sex?
How about an early feminist?
Victim of your environment? Of child abuse?
Was the closet typical Yankee discipline?
Was your enclosure prison or freedom?
Why the little girl pose, the baby, the daisy,
then taking the power in your hands?
Your face plain, your hair two red bands,
you became the Myth of Amherst.
Did you plan it? The whole show,
even your retreat into ladylike oddity?
Do you think you were mad?
Is poetry insanity? Or just yours?
Yours and William Blake's?
I agree: "Abyss is its own apology."
I understand a "revenge of the nerves,"
despair, hope, meaning, meaninglessness.
Believe me, I'm not complaining.
I can see wanting the drama, coming out
of the house in a slim white coffin.
You perfected your finale.
So, please, be straight with me
because I don't know what you mean.

A CASE OF NERVES

sweet lady
        on her collarbone welts rise
        as pink and mad as baby mice
eggshell lady
        with a fingernail she can write anyone's name
        on the inside of her arm,
        she could write *help me* if she liked
hysterical lady
        no hay lady, her breathing slows
        with the rise of the fall
thoughtful lady
        she twists through nights:
        there on the floor, the sad sheets
sleepless lady
        a pea, bad memory, bad dream:
        saving small animals, or failing
tender lady
tedious lady
        Canadian geese soothe and sadden her
        What if the ducks freeze in the river?
tremulous lady
melancholy lady
        she leads a doubled life: living
        and thinking about living,
        this is called writing
a literary lady
velvety lady
tangerine dream of a lady
        this lady should eat mangoes
        under a mango tree
mystical lady
        she should sip tepid tea
        under crimson veils and palm fronds
fantastical lady
        she's the true princess
        underneath the ordinary grime of life

typical lady
unoriginal lady
          each part of her
          is slowly weakening
impatient lady
in-patient lady
          she fears doctors,
          she fears disease
          Good God, where are her puppies?
delirious lady
          she remembers sex
          but not the feeling
temporizing lady
          her husband fills with pain,
          she's such a fine lady
featherweight lady
fair-weather friend of a lady
          they live as crazy children,
          it does them some good
terrified baby
          she's seen the pictures
caramel-cream baby of a lady
          each slight is another hive
          on the body of her life
elephant lady
lizard lady
          she remembers everything,
          catches everything
once the hyacinth girl
now a lavender lady
          her mother called her
          a delicate plant, a hothouse rose
ludicrous lady
lachrymose lady
          she feels herself
          fading, fading,
ghostly lady
          fading a little
ghastly lady
          give her a bed of rose blossoms,

            a bath of cream
            a reason
lady of the lake
            give her anxiety medication,
            she won't take it
lady of shalott
            give her a new lover,
            who dances and drinks
lady marmalade
            she does not know how
            to want this now
fragile lady
fragrant lady
            a jasmine leaf bruises her sole,
            a lemon tree weighs down her heart
            she loves all animals too much
franciscan lady
            she adores sidewalks and cafés
            but not "the blab of the pave"
discerning lady
a very particular lady
            that's the whole problem
alas: a mortal lady
            she is simply
            too fine for earth
            and heaven

STUNNER

Millais best captured your delicious passivity
        as Ophelia, your palms upended in surrender,
flowers forgotten, in those moments before
        the dress, heavy with drink, sank that mad girl.

At the last session, you lay shivering in a tub,
        the lamps underneath having run out of oil,
and caught a chill. Your father sued Millais
        for damages; he paid the doctor's bills.

Yet Rossetti's love bloomed whenever you
        flirted with death, so you kept threatening
to waste away. Consumptive? Anorexic? Another
        nineteenth-century lady with a medical mystery.

He said that his destiny was defined the instant
        he saw a milliner's assistant selling hats
to men, who took his Beatrice for an easy mark
        when she should have been in Paradise with him.

His sister criticized the use he made of you:
        "One face looks out from all his canvases,"
none of which showed a lady "wan with waiting"
        for a ring and respectability, as she knew you to be.

By the time he agreed to marry, you were lost
        to laudanum. Once wed, the artist discovered
he no longer could see his lover as his muse,
        but he did berate himself when he found you.

Home from the chophouse, stunned, drunk,
        he discarded the note pinned to your nightgown:
not suicide, just old-fashioned, accidental OD.
        He slipped a sheaf of verse under your gold hair.

Years later, having given the matter some thought,
        as the living tend to do, to the light of fires
at night, he had your body exhumed, the poems
        soaked in disinfectant and returned to the poet,

who'd sought assurance that you would still be
        "perfect," which he was determined to believe
though a wormhole shot through his "Jenny."
        When questioned by friends, Rossetti protested:

you would understand, for you loved art as he did.
        Then he burned your letters to protect
your privacy, and he burned your photographs
        because they couldn't capture your beauty.

The lasting images of you belong to the PRB.
        I have to admit, they made you lovely, nothing
like your self-portrait; the pinched face, weary
        and angry, is not, I would say, a masterpiece.

EFFIE RUSKIN, 1849

Yet another letter from John,
    calling me his "pet,"
claiming he cannot wait
    for us to reunite,

how it seems to him a dream
    that we are married;
on our "next bridal night,"
    he will lean his cheek

against my "snowy shoulders,"
    as if I had been
until then only his betrothed.
    I do not believe him.

He is touring the Continent
    with his parents again.
His imagery must come from
    all the marble Greeks.

I am not as smooth, cool,
    and poreless as a statue,
whose only hair circles like
    white rope on her head.

I have never been that immaculate,
    even as a girl. I wonder
if he would better love a child's
    body, one that is still

a bud, not an opened rose.
    I wonder if he will.
I know he has left me longing
    for another man, an artist,

not someone who dabbles
      and critiques but who paints
what he sees, who would look
      at me and find beauty.

SÉANCE

First, astral bells.
                      Odor of far away orchids.
                                              Our collective shiver.
                      One disembodied whisper.
A foot, a hand, a face
                      emerged from the cabinet.
                                              Then she stepped out,
                      fully materialized.
In fact, she seemed
                      as solid, as substantial
                                              as a living girl.
                      She allowed us
to count her heartbeats
                      and hold her tangible hand.
                                              She put her lips to our cheeks:
                      the coldest kiss
we had ever received.
                      Yet her presence stays
                                              untranslatable
                      like the inside of a pearl.
At most, we can say
                      that knowing a ghost,
                                              flesh returned to spirit,
                      spirit returned to flesh
in an ectoplasmic veil,
                      was like drinking
                                              spring water in Lemuria
                      or eating apples in Atlantis.
From the other side,
                      she brought us beauty
                                              and the end of death.

NIGHTINGALE

Not the immortal bird that made
      a dying man dream
of fading into the forest, far away
      from mortal misery
or a Byzantine machine, forged
      of gold in a golden land,
this Philomel was closer to Hardy's
      small, centennial thrush.

Our Victorian Cassandra feared
      her prophecies would go
unheeded as she was the moon
      to her family's Earth,
which saw only one lunar side,
      the other forever unknown
to their kind (they never took her
      seriously as a female priest).

In turn, she sneered at the stupor
      of her mother and sister,
Parthenope, who might tire
      if they put flowers into water,
their lives a middle-class suicide,
      deprived of any occupation
other than sitting together
      without a chance to think.

As for herself, "The Pope" wanted
      nothing to do with matrimony
since a woman must never be
      too busy to listen to a man
unless arranging his dinner,
      and mothers were let alone
solely when "suckling their fools,"
      she said, quoting Iago.

Nothing except "Widowhood,
        ill-health, or want of bread"
explained a woman working.
        She lacked these problems,
but "dilation of the heart"
        eased social obligations
after her stint in Crimea
        as the Lady with a Lamp.

This self-described terrier
        killed unmetaphorical rats
while handling drunken nurses
        who wanted to marry the men
who didn't die of dysentery;
        her devotion to duty led one
soldier to rhapsodize over kissing
        her shadow as she passed.

Yet Flo's own sister swore
        she lacked philanthropy.
"She's ambitious," Parthe hissed
        as if this were a sin;
Strachey called her an eagle,
        meaning a bird of prey,
but a nightingale sings as long
        as she still has her tongue.

WANDERING WOMB

It limps to my side:
a lump. My back,
I'm writhing.

When it lifts
to my temples, I can't
breathe or think.

Send the beast
back down
with sweet smells.

All creatures crave
cinnamon and myrrh,
don't they?

Then make me a pessary
of honeyed almonds
and bay leaves.

Now it's thirsty.
I have a desert inside me.
Flowers harden into cacti.

Give me a draft
of milk from an ass.
That should be enough.

But if the animal floats
to my throat, I'll need
juniper wine and cumin.

Pull it out of my skull
with all that's been
burned—

fleabane,
deer's horn,
and cedar resin.

I believe
that fiend
is poisoning me.

It lies behind my eyes,
making me a Gorgon
or common fishwife.

I fear I'll grow
the spurs of a cock,
I will lose my beauty.

Leech me. There,
at the neck of my uterus.
Ah, cup my breasts.

Remove
those rotten eggs.
Sew me up.

Allow me
a change of scene,
a chance to take the waters.

I'm fainting.
I can't rise from my bed.
My life is a swoon.

Take these pages. Take my pen.
They've done nothing
but trouble me.

Bring on the music
and magnetism. I'm a magician's
assistant in lavender silk.

Show me off
to your colleagues.
Let them learn from my body.

Press the points on my skin
as a child does her doll.
Mama. Papa.

Beware bicycles.
Beware horseback riding.
Beware what seems to be

the innocent tap, tap, tapping
of the foot pedal on my sewing machine.
Everything ignites desire.

Soothe me
with Miss Pinkham's vegetable tonic
or straight gin.

Lay me down
on the couch
every day at three.

Once I became
a woman, something was lost.
Something has happened to me.

Augustine, Photographed at the Salpêtrière

A spider lives in my right ear. It wants to devour the red ribbons on my neck. Then I'll no longer be pretty. If you want more, give me ether. I'm still only thirteen, Monsieur, have pity. Shall I face the camera? Where are you? I mean, in relation to me. I remember things. But it doesn't feel like remembering. What's that monster under the black cloth? It's too terrible to be seen. The eye hurts me. The eye snaps like turtles. I breathe in smoke all night after one of these sessions. It smells like hellfire. When you speak, must flames shoot from your lips that way? You're trying to frighten me. You're giving me frogs. Impossible. There's no white flow. You don't need to take my temperature. May I put on my clothes? May I wear the nurse's uniform, the one with lace? What do you know of medicine? I can't move my right leg. I'm frozen in place. I'm a photograph now, aren't I? Is that allowed? How heavy you are! The weight of angels is nothing like this. You want my secrets. Is that what the camera takes? You wish me to sin, but you're a sinner yourself. Is this a confession? What shall I write? My dorsal side? My ventral side? I don't follow you. This doesn't make sense. Please don't let there be rats. They're crawling all over your face. They seem to me nightmares. Is that right? Give me ether. Is that the Savior? Chloroform. Thank you. What does Jesus say? I am good. He loves me. You must not hurt me anymore. Sometimes I dream of leaving the hospital. I step outside, but I can't see blues or greens. Everything is black and white except roses, which remain as red as the blood on my pillow. Let's finish up now. Let's just get through this, Monsieur.

Talking Cure

"Dora" was plagued with aphasia and vaginal catarrh
after "Herr K," unwanted husband of her father's lover,
pressed himself upon her. Had she been a normal girl,
      A house was on fire.
she would have responded with the attraction natural
at fourteen, not such blunt disgust. Diagnosis: hysteria,
reversal of affect, displacement of sensation. Basically,
      *My father was standing
      beside my bed*
she was a prick tease, for her would-be seducer must have
received numerous hints that he was secure in the girl's
affections. At her father's direction, the doctor used
      and woke me up.
all his powers against his patient in the name of reason,
never flinching from exposing her fantasies in the manner
of a gynecologist uncovering every inch of the female body:
      I dressed myself quickly.
"pour faire une omelette il faut casser des oeufs." In sum,
her dream of a schmuck-kästchen expressed fascination
with female genitalia, and for this "suck-a-thumbs,"
      *Mother wanted to stop
      and save her jewel-case;*
"'No' signified the expected 'Yes.'" Maddeningly,
she "wanted to play 'secrets'" with him, "I don't know"
the way the minx admitted whatever she still repressed.
      but Father said:
      "I refuse to let myself
      and my two children be burnt
      for the sake of your jewel-case."
He knew that she awaited his kiss, having transferred her
feelings to him; if she had stayed, he could have gone
on to masturbation and latent lesbian tendencies,
      We hurried downstairs,
but she broke off unexpectedly in "an unmistakable act
of vengeance." At their final meeting, Miss Bauer at last
stopped fighting his findings. For once, she said nothing.
      *and as soon as I was outside
      I woke up.*

Lizzie Borden Bed and Breakfast Museum

In the morning, you can roll out
of bed, put your feet on the spot
where the stepmom bought it,

then descend to the dining room,
done in cheap chintz, and eat
Johnnycakes alongside muffins,

a breakfast similar to the one
(minus three-day-old mutton),
which nurtured the murder victims

on that hot day in August,
in this house with no air-
conditioning and no hallways.

What's the matter with us?
Lizzie Borden Bed and Breakfast?
True, there's little to do in Fall River.

Plus, she's a sight to see on the sidewalk,
clutching an umbrella, in mourning
but sporting four studs in each ear.

"Lizzie" protests her innocence, a joke,
a wink to the audience. We snicker
to think of her trying to buy arsenic,

the dumb-bunny tale of hunting
for a lead sinker when she hadn't
retrieved any fishing lines,

how she dawdled in the barn
long enough to eat three pears
(the kitchen boasts a "pear motif")

and chose to burn
a blue dress in the stove
three days after the deaths.

Newspapers said undoubtedly
a Portuguese, a laborer, a man did it.
So what if she profited?

Her attorney insisted the crime
was "physically and morally
impossible" for the spinster,

who got off and returned home
to a band playing "Auld Lang Syne."
That's the yuck yuck of this story.

Remove a double murder
to another century,
give us a chance

to condescend—
how naïve to assume no woman
could do that!—and sell us tickets.

We'll buy them.
We'll buy the Lizzie apron
and Lizzie paperweights.

We'll find them amusing.
They will, I mean. Those fools.
I'm only here for material,

for anything that's not the same
wretched me, the worst offender,
poet-ghoul, hungry for irony.

Mata Hari

Eastern Venus to Duncan's Vestal Virgin
 ("feline" and "feminine" purred *La Vie Parisienne*),
  the *charmante artiste* turned sexy into *tragique*
   as a thousand curves of her body
    trembled in a thousand foreign rhythms.
     An Indian diadem tucked in her hair,
      elaborately knotted à l'espagnole,
       sequinned breastplates topping
        a bejeweled waistband that held up
         the shocking sarong, she sacrificed herself
        to Shiva, letting all seven veils fall
       at the feet of her god, leaving herself
      for Paris to see. In Italy, La Scala. In Spain,
       she had been thought a goddess, she said,
        her soles not allowed to touch the ground,
         hot-blooded cavaliers throwing down
          their coats and capes for her to walk upon
           though her long-lost husband scoffed,
            "She's got flat feet and can't dance."
           What are facts in comparison to fascination?
          If a woman has the guts to forge a new identity?
         All the bulbous-nosed Dutch mother
        needed was a strange name, something
       arresting, a willingness to shake her booty
      in fabricated costumes of exotica, and enough
       nerve to criticize the inaccuracies of imitators.
        With Hindu blood bubbling in her veins,
         she brought to us, the Uninitiated West,
          sacred dances of her native India.
           She alone had been bred to comprehend
            the meaning of these ancient rites best
             performed under palm trees and moonlight;
           only she could honor their solemnity.
          Such chutzpah takes my breath away
         though many were taken in back then.

According to one dumbstruck newsman,
"the oriental woman" could not understand
　　the falsity of our commercial world
　　　　and found us hilarious. I'll bet she did.
　　　　　　As Scheherazade, she learned that tales
　　　　　　　　could keep her in furs and lovers,
　　　　　　　　　　but when Captain Bouchardon asked her
　　　　　　　　　　　　to tell the court the story of her life,
　　　　　　　　before long she faced a firing squad.
　　　　　　"Accustomed to make use of men," he said,
　　　　"she is the type of woman born to be a spy."
　　She protested, "I know nothing of your war."
　　That was men's business; all the men
she'd known had been her friends.
　　None of them listened. She met death bravely,
　　　　no longer a sister of the Nymphs, her figure
　　　　　　no one's poem, yet in Eastern garb, her pose
　　　　　　　　as the Rose, she made me believe her story,
　　　　　　　　　　or should I say I can see how someone
　　　　　　　　　　　　who wanted to could choose to believe?

Queen Alice

I stuck your picture in a Kmart frame, and there you remain
    among portraits of my family, one from a tourist spot

where the photographer pulled a barroom gown over my dress,
    propped a bonnet on my head, and handed me a parasol,

my husband a top hat and long coat, a cane. She was pleased
    to see he had on pants since shorts made the illusion

that much harder to create. Done in "sepia," I look great,
    at home in my duds, a smug madam; Chris, shy and young.

Wedding photos show off another imitation Victorian get-up,
    a long-awaited prom dress dug out of the racks at the mall.

Behind this, a black and white studio shot of my siblings and me:
    Michael in a Disneyland T-shirt; angelic Cheryl, a little cross

around her throat; Jerry, shrinking within himself but happy
    to be in his cowboy outfit; and an Alfred Hitchcock baby,

unmistakable shock in my camera-locked eyes. *The horror, the horror.*
    No wonder I added you to my history although all I saw

when I found you in a dead person's scrapbook was the ancestor
    of my Pomeranian, and a young woman, with a strong jaw,

whose cameo was at odds with the psychedelic pattern of her dress—
    uneven globules dancing crazily down the arms and waist.

Hidden as a girl with your stepmother, "like houris in a harem,"
    as men danced the "stately minuet" of male-run government,

you'd become the most photographed person on the planet,
    smoking stolen cigarettes on the roof of the White House,

getting caught paying off a bookie at the track, wearing flesh-
    colored stockings (ladies wore black), tucking up your sleeves

copies of the Constitution and flasks of bourbon during Prohibition,
    bopping to the scandalous Turkey Trot, sniffing that Franklin

never went to the really good parties, and eschewing Eleanor's piety.
    For your wedding, you requested trinkets, preferably diamond,

and attended more dances in a single year than there are days,
    once done up like a wealthy Cinderella in heels of cut glass.

You lived long enough to see Pound at St. Elizabeth's, to chastise
    McCarthy, to get my reference to LSD, to witness the deaths

of the aristocratic, if democratic, Kennedys, then Watergate,
    which produced "amusing TV." "The only topless octogenarian

in Washington" after a double mastectomy, a "withered Twiggy,"
    you could still sink into a full lotus and dismiss your famous kin

as "upstart Dutch who made a couple of bucks." Of yourself: "Perhaps
    I'll be a footnote." No, my dear, not for those who hope for more.

Teacher

The woman trapped in a statue,
       cast in plaster as the living dead,
             her connections scent and flesh,
all other portals blocked with cement,
       became our marvel and brain-tease.
             As a girl, she'd been a beast,
lost in "the tangible white darkness,"
       with only a few gestures to ask
             for contact (Father: glasses;
Mother: hand to her cheek).
       But she grew unfairly beautiful,
             eyes swapped for blue glass,
although something remained
       disconnected, cut off, in the face
             posed with survivors in Hiroshima,
encircled by Martha Graham's dancers,
       and on the vaudeville stage alongside
             Jack Johnson, who showed photos
of his wife's funeral, or the lesser known
       "Human Tank," who swallowed frogs
             whole and threw them up alive.
Befriended by Bell and Twain, she'd be
       hailed the eighth wonder of the world,
             a world that stayed for her,
she confessed, an "imaginary construction,"
       based on "the fallen angels" of smell
             and touch, a rough translation of us.
She stole language from Earthlings
       to take back to Venus. Another
             woman had to give her life
for the fusion necessary to break
       through those walls and find a soul,
             but this forceful Irish girl,
Helen's "other self," a bully in love
       with her creation, as creators will be,

     led her pupil to that moment
(black obelisk, moon launch, silicon chip)
    when she pumped into a cupped hand
      and offered her the word, *water,*
a gift for which she received in return
    what the rest of us want: that moment
      (genetic code, penicillin, relativity)
when a student understands at last,
   then wants to know who we are,
     and we can answer, "Teacher."

Flapper

Shrinks said, *Inferiority complex.* Yes,
        dilettantes can be a pain in the ass.

Still, Zelda, Scott's cyclone, his only god,
        there's something to be said for being

a personality, your greatest creation the girl
        who didn't give a fig for respectability

and caused scenes, stewed at parties,
        before you got off the sauce for good,

nothing but whole milk and sanitariums
        after you cracked up too badly to mend,

then turned into the cuckoo, the mad widow,
        in the end identified by a charred slipper.

Listen, ripping that much life out of youth
        is quite an accomplishment too.

BLOOD IN LONDON

The smoky essence
Within those yellowed rooms
And all along the avenues
Is, you must admit, a feminine perfume.

I think of African masks and Grecian friezes.
Something ancient and awful arises and sneezes.

It does not matter
If one opens the shutters,
If one holds one's head and mutters,
  I am above this.

Let me not drag through the streets again.
Let no jingles and grins jolt me into life again.

If she were to hang
Upside down, my beautiful chiroptera,
With lilac lips and paling knees,
We might be all right.

If she were to lie
In a coffin of glass, a timeless slice of apple
Lodged in a white throat, hands gloves of ice,
I'd watch over la Belle Dormant
With my Mandarin smile.
I'd sail us into eternity.

Far out on the water is a fire . . .
Dämmerung der Götter. Valhalla?
Comitatus, let the mead flow. Wait for me.

Inside, the candles hiss and fizzle.
Another leg of mutton, love,
Another conversation.

The Afflicted Girls

If we were submarine dwellers
In a green world, I would ring her
Fingers with seaweed and bless her
Face as it sank away from mine,
Each word another bubble
Dissolving on the surface.
This is the right sort of talk
Between a woman and a man
In a slowly enclosing evening.

But the teacups clatter ceaselessly.
A new butter dish, she says,
A butter dish is what we need.

Had there been a baby,
It might have had bat wings.
It might have flown freely into the violet night,
Leaving us with greater longing.

In the sea, coral
Slices men to ribbons.
No soul can wade into shore.

In London, blood and bills,
Doctors with myriad queries
And myriad theories but little help.

How many ways can a lady be ill?
By Christ, she shall find them all.

Outside, girls laugh
As if the universe were possible.
For a minute, I am abashed.

How might I say, *I only see you in pieces,*
Yet it's better this way. Afternoons,
She lays her palm upon mine,
Full of wine and violins. I will a smile.
This should last a little while.

No, no, no.
Chattering, chattering,
Off to bed we go.

There's the church,
       there the gutter:
We're alone with the wind,
       or muddily together.

In marriage there can be no division.
   This is one of her decrees.
I assure her I cannot envision
   God offering any such reprieves.

Flames lick her skin—This is my wife.
I have burnt my boats for such a wraith.
       Le coeur a ses raisons.
       Militat omnis amans.

Is it five o'clock yet?
Shall I turn on the light?
Dull percussion pounds my brain.
Tom, tom, tom. Is it her heart?
Or the flow between her legs?

After it's over, the usual apologies.
May I stay with you tonight?
Shall we have our tea then? In here . . . or?
As though we might even now be pleased.
As if we might call back that hour
On the beach when we knew nothing
Of the other, both perfectly incomplete.

Once she was my river girl,
Drenched with rain and shimmering.

Such is the treachery of love.
I confess, I am not well myself.

New Yorker

At the Gonk, whiskey and White Rock
        Conquered Chypre and dog shit
As you showed that love was a crock
        And made the most of your wit.

But after the rams came the blues;
        Even your light rhymes grew dark,
And Death waited for you to choose
        Heaven, Hell, or Central Park.

La Gran Ocultadora

Daughter of the Revolution, you made yourself into a human *piñata*
in solidarity with *las soldaderas,* even *los pelados,* dressed in *Mexique*
costumes adorned with peasant lace and pre-Colombian jewelry

that would have pleased an Aztec queen or the goddess Xochitl,
the cracked column of your spine encased in corsets and braces.
Laughing with *carcajadas,* you were half-serious and half-joking.

Not sick, badly broken, you were also *la chingada,* the screwed one,
pata de palo, love's wounded dove wed to an elephant, old man Diego,
el macho, the maestro, whose murals loomed over American factories,

who said the more he loved women the more he wanted to hurt them,
but you didn't take on Rivera's pageantry or the usual female nudes,
only you, a face mustachioed and indifferent above a disintegrating body.

Painter and painted, your palette a heart, brushes dripping blood,
you stared into a mirror to turn your insides out. As a Tehuana bride
or wounded deer bearing a necklace of thorns, monkey by your side,

tied to fruits and parrots with vines or veins, you showed your life
to be *un mar de làgrimas*. Gotten up in the regular regalia but not able
to stand a mirror anymore, you turned to still life, *naturaleza muerta*.

Muertes en relajo: the dead having a last fling. It's your great pain
that intrigues me, a gringa living in "gringolandia," yet I am more
taken by how you showed the snails on the underside of your rose.

I wish I could give you *milagros* for the foot life stole, sweets, brandy,
a doll to hold, a baby at last, *chiquita, la bailarina,* since you lost both
virginity and motherhood to the metal handrail, torn open in the street,

but wonderfully covered with the gold dust carried by another passenger,
an artisan, your pain already a painting. I hope your exit was as joyful
as you'd hoped and that you never have to come back this way again.

Fairy Tale

Everyone knows
who the witch is.

We've seen her
dropping her kids off at daycare.

She's the anesthesiologist
who hires a British au pair.

She's the teacher
who gives you a D.

She's the woman
who isn't smiling.

A pretty thing
into cigarettes and barbiturates
failed at suburban housewifery.
Her children ran off
with their grandmother.
Her husband swam in his own pool of gin.
Their cottage creaked open
like a Cape Cod beach shack.
It moaned, "Love me, love me,"
on summer mornings.
In the winter, it stayed in a trance.

The witch is mad.
She's froot loops.
She's dingdong nuts.
Besides, she's not the brightest bulb
in our poetic chandelier.
She can't remember anything.
She's been alone too long
in her red nightie.

The Afflicted Girls

In the old days,
she bedded the milkman,
the mailman, the guy from UPS.
Witches drive men crazy.
Then witches drive men crazy.
"Love me, love me,"
on summer mornings.
In the winter, a trance.

She's grown lonely as a flasher,
as a sheep rancher,
as an underpaid parlor maid.
She has been dreaming
of the splashy disappearances
of sister witches,
how they clawed their way
to that moon.
She types out her own death warrant:

A boy and a girl,
brother and sister,
two pumpkin seeds,
jog into the forest
with seven finger-puppets,
a bottle of their father's homebrew,
and a number of questions.
Little Ingrid and Petrovich
punch each other's stomachs
with the puppets sewn
by their put-upon stepmother.
They throw their bottle
through the witch's window
though no glass shatters.
There is no glass.
The damn bottle lands in her lap.
Petrovich pokes his head in.
Mr. Inquisitor.

The witch is as thin as a model,
her growl theatrical.

She takes him into her starving arms
and calls him Little Richard,
sweet gherkin,
final folly.
She diddles his pizzle
and asks him to paddle
on top of her,
a boat lost at sea.
He does what he's told.
He's a good boy.
He plants his seed.
Yet her uterus is blessed with emptiness.
There's no way around this.
She's in her forties.
She writes him fourteen poems
when he leaves her
to sleep off the beer buzz.
The witch tongues another tranquilizer,
ocean eyes on the moon.
"I'm a circus freak," she says.
"God's little Jesus."

"Love me, love me,"
Ingrid pipes up.
"Love me, love, me,"
the witch moans
into her cooling soup.
Ingrid nestles into her neck
until the witch cuddles the girl,
feeling the matching fingertips,
mother-of-pearl rosary,
ruby nipples,
and finds the peach-divide
of her daughter's body,
eating the child out
of the woman,
her rival,
her devotee,
her replacement.

CONFESSION TO THE MOON

> *last extant poem—unfinished*
> *(annotated by the poet's husband)*

Black rook, black pond.
Havoc of an autumn moon,
ghostly wood-smoke in the fen
        [Omission]
false morels linger beside
iced and dying bellwort,
incandescent at midnight
        [a minor incident
        became magnified in her mind
        to gigantic proportions]
wayward and rustic,
miracle in blood.
Thundering, full of God,
        [nothing like this
        happened to us]
clay heads roll dully
over one golden curl, the girl
genius, blitzkrieg of imagery
        [here she mocks the work
        of her more famous husband]
He comes, hulking, huge,
mother lode in a low mist.
Slam shut, old door, father death
        [a diatribe against her husband
        whom, by all accounts, she loved]
Grecian, Roman,
milk-breasts turned
to stone, I have frozen
        [she also loved her children]
bliss, a new Titan
walks upon the land
and wakes Isis

> [her husband spooned
> in chicken soup
> when she had the flu]

not sun-sick
but moon-soaked, I breathe
powerful blooms,
> [depressed over her
> husband's latest success]

His mouth an opening of the rose
to infinity
> [flowers always sank her
> into another funk]

ready at last to
> [omission]

luscious worm on my lips—
> [continued in one
> of the missing journals]

Immortal/mortal.
His marble and flesh chest
> [another swipe
> at men in general]

rising, unmoored, holy,
I sing three words
to remake the world:
> [ending emended]

winter covers all.

SUICIDE'S DAUGHTER

A New England princess
Ran bang smash into love

With a British king.
That's how you framed it, isn't it?

Rich with womanhood!
No virgin! Not barren!

But you quailed at the alien within,
Seasick on the shore of our realm.

You slipped your moorings
And rocked away

In a boat full of holes,
Searching for Neptune.

Oh, you, with your fifties' truths,
Academic vocabulary,

Tortured images, and *that accent*.
Half Brit, half Smith.

Rainbow flag's flying, Mom.
A hotbed of lesbians.

What would you have thought?
What would you have done?

Vaporous jellyfish.
Sunken treasure.

Might you have sipped
Old-Fashioneds at the Ritz

With blue-blooded ladies?
Grown complacent on Prozac?

Lived to dance at my wedding?
I could have been your friend,

No longer rope on your soul,
My fists not just red knots

When you dreamed of the deep.
Freedom-fighter, you missed it.

Tripping in the Summer of Love.
Seventies movies. Eighties techno-pop.

In the nineties, grunge.
Even the millennium.

Nothing but mud in your lungs.
Mother, you had your moment

When technique met tragedy,
And you turned into *then*.

JAYNE MANSFIELD AND ISADORA DUNCAN

Heedlessly, Isadora let her breathtaking scarf
        buckle in the breeze until it looped around one
                of the wheels of the Bugatti, breaking her neck,

and Jayne, a B version of Marilyn, more overdone
        without the underlying tristesse, stayed cartoonish
                even in death, practically decapitated in her Caddy:

what lessons can we learn here, my dears? Be careful
        with convertibles and accoutrements. If you must die,
                as I'm told you must, don't do so looking ridiculous.

À LA MODE

"The Birth of Venus,"
    Renoir, Raphael, Rubens,
        the waif, the vamp, the flapper,
            the Gibson girl, the Vargas girl, the Venus
                of Willendorf, the Madonna, Madonna,
                    Glenda, Gidget, Gwyneth Paltrow,
                la Gioconda, Jane Wyman, Jean Harlow,
            Tab, Fresca, Sweet 'N Low,
        Venus of Urbino's full belly,
    Degas' painful ballerinas,
Ingre's "Grande Odalisque"
    (with those spinal impossibilities),
        liposuction, total laser resurfacing,
            36-24-36, the Toronto Trim,
                Shrimpton, Yardley, Piccadilly,
                    Prada, Gucci, Modigliani,
                pinup, pinstripe, permanent make-up,
            false eyelashes, button nose, sex kitten,
        pillbox hat, Jackie O, glamour is in,
        hourglass figure, merry widow,
hoop skirt, poodle skirt, side slit,
    shag, wedge cut, French twist,
        platform shoes and stilettos,
            all you need is a handful,
                if you can pinch more than an inch,
                    don't laugh, don't frown, don't squint,
                cocoa butter, Coppertone, sunscreen,
            tanning beds, friends of Ana,
        go-go boots, hot pants, body paint,
    Scarlett O'Hara's 17" waist,
let's staple our stomachs, wire shut
    our mouths, paralyze our nerves
        (Do You Look Tired? Angry?),
            straighten our hair, shave our hairlines,
                bleach our anuses for total rectal beauty,

wear a bustle, corset, girdle, Spanks,
remove our lower ribs, swallow lye
to drain color from our blushes,
inject silicone, rooster combs, the skin
of a dead woman, bind our feet,
tattoo roses high on our thighs,
buy ourselves blue eyes,
a tummy tuck, boob job, butt lift,
Madison Avenue, Rodeo Drive, Wall Street,
Mae West, Twiggy, Beyoncé,
ThighMaster, Zumba, Pilates,
Pretty Baby, Bubble Barbie,
Bardot, Betty Boop, Clara Bow,
sunlit stunners of the PRB,
Brazilian wax, size zero, spit curl,
Fendi, Vera Wang, Helmut Lang,
A-line, formfitting, unisex,
little black dress, sleeveless, backless,
red ribbon, *à la victimé*, wound about the throat,
hair worn *à la sacrificé*—brushed forward
like a martyr's at the guillotine,
dropped neck and dropped waist,
blondes have more fun,
mini, maxi, midi,
Greta Garbo's mystery:
this is the look for spring.

The Breast Monologues

Jean Harlow's in *Platinum Blonde*

It's before the Code, so we keep rhythm as she walks. We're the real thing, not like her cotton-candy hair and drawn-on brows. She sounds like a cartoon, words clicking fast on her tongue, rat-a-tat-tat, like the chatter of a gum-snapper, a bimbo, a film actress. We know this and see how we contradict it. What's more elegant than the two of us in evening wear? Maybe that mound of Venus, defined in its own right on the big screen.

Jane Russell's in *His Kind of Woman*

Missiles, that's what we are. We can knock out your eyes. Like an erection, we point which way to go; we guide jet fighters onto ships. The most the waist can do after us is suck itself in. There's nothing left for the ass, which flattens in defeat. You don't want to unleash these puppies, Mister. That's for damn sure. We're woman to your man, but you better be man enough for us.

Marilyn Monroe's in *The Seven Year Itch*

She's all about roundness, even the white curls and the tip of her nose, so we fit in well. We're as voluptuous as cheeseburgers and vanilla shakes. We think more is more. The hips agree. We bounce; they jiggle. She tips in her slingbacks like a drunken angel. The lips agree, trembling as though she's made of buttercream. We're not sure what to make of the eyes. They have nothing to do with us. Wait a minute. Are we the cause of their despondence?

Jane Fonda's in *Klute*

Sitting low on her chest, we're as sad as she is, as sad as her shag. This is the seventies. No one smiles. Everything's a little depressing, including happiness. Sometimes she leaves birds' nests on either side of us. That's fine. We're into nature. Earth tones. We wouldn't know what to do with neon pink Lycra. She feeds us bean sprouts and tea with honey. She'll never pump us up, thank God. We'll never become *aerobic*.

Miss Bishop Has Left the Building

Everything's arranged. I have the map,
I have the key. "Here's Florida," I say.
"There's Brazil." "Boring," they tell me.

My anecdotes soon spin out of control:
A closet lesbian, isn't that interesting?
A drunk? Mad mother? Bad childhood?

Sad to say, the ol' possum didn't
Commit suicide. Too reserved, a lady.
"Listen to the tone," I say. "The irony."

They don't listen. They don't like irony.
They're into feeling. They go for blood,
Drugs, and semen. They like *Bukowski*.

"Don't you know how much work it takes
To create such beautifully contained worlds,
To seed the heavens and hang hammocks,

The sunsets warm, if foreign, the moon
Smiling behind manners at tanagers
And pelicans and self-importance?"

I say, shaking out the small, striped flags,
The brightly colored, irrelevant currency.
"No work should go into writing poetry,"

They say. They are a mob, a democracy.
My expertise is elitist and imaginary.
Oh, why must they have their own taste

When I am willing to give them mine?
"She may not be your cup of tea now,"
I say. "Maybe someday she will be."

Suddenly, I have become their mother,
And the lovely Miss Bishop lima beans.
I don't know if I can still teach, but I am

Not ready to pack it in just yet, so I put
Students into groups to analyze "motifs."
At last, they seem animated and happy.

Or are they laughing at the class? At me?
They're awfully cheerful for three o'clock,
But when I come close to their huddles,

They lapse into silence, gaping at the pages.
I fold up my notes, foregoing my exegesis
Of her pink goat and moose in moonlight.

Swallowing a single, subterranean tear,
I'm thinking, *TGIF, baby*, but I say,
"You know what old E.B. would say?

Let's end class early and get a drink."
They slap down their books. Hurray!
They like her a little better already.

FLORIDA

The prettiest state,
said my friend Elizabeth.
Or was it the prettiest name?

Either way, Florida has to be
warmer than Troy,
Michigan.

What birds live in Florida?
Are there alligators and crocodiles
shedding tears?

Are there orangutans?
Are there chimpanzees?
Do you think they're crying?

Florida,
land of hanging chads
and immigrants.

Remember that woman?
Her face like a dragon's.
Bush league.

In Florida,
does a woman dream
of Michigan?

Florida,
that stupid boot,
banana republic.

There was a girl.
Remember her?
A slut, a cigarette pig.

The Afflicted Girls

She had a baby at fourteen,
then lived in the woods
at the end of her street.

Flint, Detroit, Lansing.
What does it mean
to throw a girl away?

She hoped to take her girl
to SeaWorld. Why not shoot
for Epcot? Killer whales?

My friend Elizabeth
also liked to drink herself
into oblivion in exotic locales.

Of what did Elizabeth dream?
Toucans? Manatees? The drowned
skirt of an Indian princess.

A state of pink shirts and flamingoes.
What if Florida broke away,
floated into Cuba?

What lies in the water?
Eyes of dead bikers,
opalescent and semiprecious?

It's the sunshine state, okay.
But are there egrets? Pelicans?
Birds of paradise?

One speaks of Floridians
as if they were a bright kind
of amphibian . . .

Of what does a girl
in the woods dream?
Pepsi and Moon Pies.

Driving off in El Dorados,
Coupe de Villes,
Pontiac Sunbirds.

Blowing men.
Doing men for money.
Blowing men away.

People just started messin' with me . . .
they just started comin'
like flies on shit.

Are there anacondas in Florida?
Are there orange groves?
Are there guns?

After seven
dead men, of what
does a woman dream?

Embedded my flesh
and soul with deep inequity . . . .
You sabotaged my ass, society.

Her last meal:
KFC and French fries
(twenty dollar maximum).

Dawn
took her ashes
back to Michigan.

Taint my blood with yours.
Translate me through the star board
and bring me home eternal ever more.

Does Florida have
the praying mantis?
Scorpion? Coral snake?

Can you swim
with dolphins? How much
does it hurt them if you do?

What do you think
they put into your veins in Florida?
The tears of an Indian princess?

Molly Finn, Taken by the Sea

Who dies that kind of death these days?
It's the twenty-first century.

People do though.
They do in Rhode Island.

I see the widows' pictures in the paper.
Wives of missing fishermen,

in black scarves, beat their chests,
their lament and lost men timeless.

But not a girl of nineteen,
not your Molly Finn.

She'd already gone
as far as California and Australia.

Why join the crew of a ship
christened *Free Spirit*?

Was this her way of standing
in the rain and calling down lightning?

Where was she going?
No one knew for sure.

The Azores, Europe, perhaps farther.
A girl like that can go forever.

The language of rescue
is beautiful and precise.

Nautical miles. Knots.
Distress call. Debris field.

From the coast of Nova Scotia
came a Halifax frigate

along with helicopters named
Jay Hawks and Sea Kings

as if with the right words
we can rule everything.

Nothing is worse than calling it off,
said the head of the search.

It's the awesome decision
to let the astronaut drift into darkness

or abandon the baby in the bulrushes.
It's telling the family, *Your daughter*

is gone, gone your Molly Finn.
She may be the stars and the wind,

but she's never coming home again,
not as your own Molly Finn.

OCEAN STATE

Isn't that heaven then?
To die and be more fully alive?

Her heart, they swore,
had engorged with blood.

What can a family do?
Cut out their girl's heart.

Feed it to the ailing son
though this too won't cure him.

Burn her heart.
Mix the ashes with an elixir

in Exeter, Rhode Island, where
consumption ruled the day,

where an Englishman's bones
have just been found.

He'd flown in from London
to meet a Bostonian.

Sexual asphyxiation,
they suspect.

How far we're willing to go
for sex, for love.

To Wickford, we fled,
illicit then and limerent,

but my husband doesn't love
Heathcliff and his Cathy.

He thinks of Mr. Sardonicus. He thinks
of Lizzie Siddal and Rossetti's poetry.

I am waiting and watching for you,
says the headstone of Nelly Vaughn.

Horseman, pass by! says Yeats' grave,
for he was a great poet.

We want our loved ones to return
to us in blown dandelions or rainbows

or the song of the robin
outside our window

but not as the hand on the doorknob,
not as the teeth in our neck,

so they burned their girl's heart on a rock,
New England's best crop.

My dog's ashes feed our garden,
but I didn't eat his heart.

My mother's ashes feed the fishes
of the Pacific. Hers either.

I ask for presents after I'm dead.
I ask for undying fidelity.

My husband supposes I'm joking,
that I'm not Mercy Brown.

Yet don't the dead always
consume the living?

Love, I tell my husband, let go
of my ashes but hold onto my poems.

Teen Vamp

Its like
first i was any other
Goth chick nothing but black
lipstick & shit (friggin poser!)—
all RPG, a wannabe but i grew
ever more attached to the Night
whilst my poetry got really dark & deep.

> *Crystal midnight*
> *cresendoing goblets*
> *your Alabaster stallion*
> *my sinister Passion*

Than i cant stand sunlight
or mornings or my mom whos all like
get up already what are you
the living dead & im like well
may be i am, ive always been
really mystical in my thinking
(open to new things)

> *The Lady of Spades*
> *holds a crimson key*
> *to savage love*
> *with Elvish Kings*

Faes are alright. Therianthropes too.
(noone says werewolfs now a days.)
ive nothing against wikans or satanists.
Some are really nice people!
& will let you sit at there table
unlike some people i could mention.
(Jon Tunney Shakira Carpenter Jen Greene)

> *Ruby lips drip rivers*
> *of desire which is*
> *vermelion hell fire*
> *in my Burning Brain.*

At sixteen i had my Awakening.
Than im all like PSI vamping—

at the food court i could suck someone
dry a hundred feet away from me.
Their tacobelling while im munching
there "prana" which means energy
(scientificly really proven to exist.)

> *Ivory fangs flash*
> *in the sweet dying*
> *of an Ebony dawn*
> *unleashing garnet tears . . . .*

Than im doing V8 & rare stakes
to stave off the anchent Thirst
but soon my kid sisters bunny
Mista Whiskas is looking
really yummy so i buy me
a set of killer fangs on Ebay
& find my first (wilful) donor.

> *Dancing & Turning*
> *im hunting, im yearning*
> *your bare necks alluring*
> *my Vortex is Churning.*

The teeth dont work that great
so Kevin Shaunessey sex fiend
lets me take a razor to his skin.
Like the Bible says "blood is life"
& boy that Kevin Shaunessy
really hit the spot. Dont worry!
Hes alright. (he got laid & all)

> *Droplets of red Droplets of white*
> *one is Death one is Life*
> *who can tell wrong from right?*
> *Welcome to reality.*

Its not the romance of the centurys.
Kevins just a suck buddy he calls
me blood junky, i call him chicken.
Hell only have a few scars from this
which is really like his contribution
to creatures of darkness—meaning
me, Amy (DeadlyBNghtShade).

Stolen moments & Silver veins
one scarlet kiss
ignites an eclipse & stains
are Eternal Embrace

So now i know what i am—
a Sagitarian & a Sanguinarian.
Accept my familys Lutheran
& really freaked by me!
Being immortals tough its no picnic.
Its not like those stupid movies.
Everyone will die while i keep living.

O how I yearn
for the Long Nights of Old
angelicas & dragons & me—
their Vampyre Queene!

Its not like i think
im a princess the way my parents mean.
im sorry im not human like them
(with there mundane existense).
Some of us are born to be more
then that, some of us are just
like really diffrent.

HITHERTO UNDISCLOSED CATEGORIES OF UNFORTUNATE DEMISE

> *LONDON (AP) 2011—Coroner Suzanne Greenaway gave a verdict of "death by misadventure"...*

Misalignment of tires or chakras
Misalliance with a door-to-door salesman
Misapplication of mathematical principles
Misapprehension of either time or place
Misappropriation of others' husbands
Miscellany from the eighteenth century
Mischance—as in gaming or cakes
Misconduct of an extreme nature
Miscreants or other malingering malefactors of maledictions
Misdiagnosis by medical doctors or so-called "doctors of philosophy"
Mishap (happens all the time)
Misjudgment regarding heights, helium, or heavyweights
Mislabeling that leads to improper dosage or internet dating
Misplacement of one's priorities
Misrule, the lord of
Missed chances (don't get me started)
Miss Havisham
Missiles, Cuban or any other kind
Missives hidden under rugs or delivered
Miss, Swiss
mistake—for that is human nature
Mister Tingles
Mistletoe (see *The Pain of Love*)
Mistranslation from the French
Mistreatment of whales or women at SeaWorld
Mistress (between "mister" and "mattress")
Mistrial and just desserts
Mistrust of one's own heartbeat
Misty (in Irish songs or of the eyes)
Misunderstanding between friends (aka amusing adversaries)
Misusage (see *pet endearments*)
Mysterious circumstances

Mystery novel (literary absorption)
Mystical crystals
Mystic, Connecticut
Myths: Greek, Christian, or "personal" regarding the meaning of death or chicken-fried steak

MASH UP: RUSH MEETS FERAL PIGS IN THE CHAMPLAIN VALLEY

wily elusive foragers
hunt at night

picking cornstalks clean
making off with apple crops

so much sex
long plagued

the peaceful Champlain Valley
random hook-ups with these babes

wild boars
not the gentle, pink cousins

rarely spotted
they roam by night

steer clear
sex life is active

at any time and in any number
so much sex that it's hard to make ends meet

eyes eerily aglow in the light of the flash
they want to have sex anytime

who knows where they'll end up?
hunt them from Hawaii to Alabama

what do you call them?
what does that make her?

having sex so frequently
I'm out of money

a real sense of urgency
"sounder" in swine-speak

the pigs here have grown wary
I've never seen an animal this smart

it's not fair
they're lined up around the block

post the videos online so we can all watch
voracious and vicious and the bane of farmers

they'll eat the understory
then we want something in return.

Skin

like the Fat Lady
like the Bearded Lady
like the startling Spidora, Illusionist Extraordinaire

butterfly parts her wings
shaved head sprayed gold
tongue studs, labia rings

"I Live and Die for Those I Love"

floral necklaces dipping into cleavage
angels and dolphins, corporate logos
hives of bees, bands of fairies

teardrops, man's ruin, rosaries
zippers running up the spine
necks laced and tied with a yellow bow

"Nothing Without Labor"

on my back, chinese dragons
thorns embrace both ankles
my arms the same, with my boyfriend's name

like that shriveled egyptian princess
like lady churchill, hiding her symbol of infinity
like Janis Joplin, heart upon her heavy chest

"Never Give In"

we're all going to die
why can't our bodies be
objects of beauty

THE PRINCESS BRIDE

You took pride in being hard-hitting, unsparing, mostly of
    yourself, of your complicity
in the daily disasters of marginal lives during the sixties and
    seventies, that dark carnival of desire and despair,
as you measured Wisconsin's emptiness, a drunken father,
    weakened mother,
bringing together nuns, medieval paintings, and Jane Austen
with the Blues Rock Bar, Pabst Blue Ribbon, all the trappings of
    bad girls
through a relentless accumulation of details, from "hand-stacked
    wheat" to "homegrown weed heavy with seeds."
In verse, you're one tough honey, presiding over the inferno of
    blue-collar bars and misalliances,
yet you agreed to watch *The Princess Bride* with me.
You said I kept you in touch with the mainstream, but you said it
    lightly.
You were forgiving. You were funny. You were in the middle of
    your story at forty,
newly blond and sleeping with men again after many years with
    women.
Who knows what you would have done next,
what you would have made of the fluid seeping into your lungs,
limping home to the Midwest, sitting outside on the one warm day
    in November and brushing away all the loose strands of
    yellow hair.
I'm sorry. I'm not fighting fair. Indulge me.
As fine as your poems are, they lie, so here I am, shouting, "She
    was kind, the best of friends,"
even though you weaseled me into driving from Houston to San
    Francisco, mid-June, in an ancient Civic with no AC,
your hair silver then, mine stuck with fifty bobby pins under a red
    bandanna (imagine!),
waking to find New Mexico purple in the morning. When we went
    to bed
in a cut-rate motel, you rubbed your feet together under the

    sheets, like a grasshopper singing, until I told you to knock
        it off.
Of my long, unhappy liaison with a man, you said, "Miss Calbert,
        the truth is we'll do anything for love."
This is one that I've done.

"Ophelia" (1910) by John William Waterhouse (1849 -1917)

Notes

The following sources were extremely helpful in providing background information and quotations for the poems in this volume:

First Wife (Lilith): Siegmund Hurwitz's *Lilith: The First Eve*.

Assumption (Mary): Michael P. Carroll's *The Cult of the Virgin Mary: Psychological Origins*; Marina Warner's *Alone of All Her Sex: The Myth and Cult of the Virgin Mary*.

Sainted Ladies of the Middle Ages: Caroline Walker's *Holy Feast and Holy Fast*. Various female saints reportedly made some of the statements in the poem.

Heretic: Frances Geis's *Joan of Arc: The Legend and the Reality*.

The Afflicted Girls: John Putnam Demos's *Entertaining Satan*; Carol F. Carlsen's *The Devil in the Shape of a Woman*. Some of the language in the poem derives from depositions given by young women involved in the witch trials at Salem.

The Wild Girl of Champagne: Julia Douthwaite's "Rewriting the Savage: The Extraordinary Fictions of the 'Wild Girl of Champagne.'"

Pirating (Anne Bonny): Captain Charles Johnson's *A General History of the Robberies and Murders of the most notorious Pyrates, and also Their Policies, Discipline and Government,* *from their First Rise and Settlement in the Island of Providence, in 1717, to the present year 1724.*

Genius: Susan M. Levin's *Dorothy Wordsworth and Romanticism*; Dorothy Wordsworth's *The Grasmere Journals*.

At Chawton Cottage: Jane Austen's *Letters to her Sister Cassandra and Others*, collected and edited by R.W. Chapman. Some word choices in the poem are Austen's own.

The Lambs (Mary Lamb): E.V. Lucas' *The Life of Charles Lamb*. Samuel Taylor Coleridge is the speaker of the poem.

"The Misses Bronte's Establishment for The Board and Education of a Limited Number of Young Ladies": Katherine Frank's *A Chainless Soul: A Life of Emily Brontë*. The title comes from Charlotte Brontë's proposed advertisement for a boarding school she rather madly hoped to open with her sisters. The last sentence is from Emily Brontë's diary and the earliest reference to the sisters' imagined kingdom.

Motherhood: Mardy S. Ireland's *Reconceiving Women: Separating Motherhood from Female Identity*; Nancy Chodorow's *The Reproduction of Mothering*; Ann Dally's *Inventing Motherhood: The Consequences of an Ideal*; Adrienne Rich's *Of Woman Born*; *Between Ourselves: Letters Between Mothers and Daughters*, edited by Karen Payne.

Dear Miss Dickinson, is my letter to the woman who never wrote to me.

A Case of Nerves: Elaine Showalter's *The Female Malady*.

Stunner (Elizabeth Siddal): Gay Daly's *Pre-Raphaelites in Love*. "Jenny" is a poem by Rossetti.

Effie Ruskin, 1849: Daly's *Pre-Raphaelites in Love*; Phyllis Rose's *Parallel Lives: Five Victorian Marriages*.

Séance is inspired by the "spirit" Katie King.

Nightingale: F.B. Smith's *Florence Nightingale: Reputation and Power; Ever Yours, Florence Nightingale: Selected Letters.*

Wandering Womb: Sarah Stage's *Female Complaints: Lydia Pinkham and the Business of Women's Medicine*; Mark S. Micale's *Hysteria: The History of a Disease*; Ilza Veith's *Approaching Hysteria: Disease and Its Interpretations.*

Augustine, Photographed at the Salpêtrière: Georges Didi-Huberman's *Invention of Hysteria: Charcot and the Photographic Iconography of the Salpêtrière*, translated by Alisa Hartz. Some statements attributed to Augustine in the poem derive from transcripts included in this translation.

Talking Cure (Ida Bauer): Sigmund Freud's *Dora: An Analysis of a Case of Hysteria*, edited by Philip Rieff. The right-hand column comes from Freud's summary of a dream Bauer recounted to him.

Lizzie Borden Bed and Breakfast Museum was recently for sale, but I did not buy it.

Mata Hari: Sam Waagenaar's *Mata Hari.*

Queen Alice: Howard Teichmann's *Alice: The Life and Times of Alice Roosevelt Longworth*; Michael Teague's *Mrs. L: Conversations with Alice Roosevelt Longworth.*

Teacher (Annie Sullivan): Dorothy Herrmann's *Helen Keller: A Life*; Helen Keller's *The Story of My Life.*

Flapper (Zelda Sayres Fitzgerald): Nancy Milford's *Zelda: a Biography.*

Blood in London: Carole Seymour-Jones' *Painted Shadow: The Life of Vivienne Eliot, First Wife of T.S. Eliot.*

New Yorker (Dorothy Parker). I wish I'd attended the parties.

La Gran Ocultadora: Hayden Herrera's *Frida: A Biography of Frida*

Kahlo; *The Diary of Frida Kahlo: An Intimate Self-Portrait*. Kahlo referred to herself as "la gran ocultadora." She wrote in her last diary entry about hoping for a joyful exit and never coming back.

Fairy Tale (Anne Sexton). The poem roughly follows the poetic strategies of Sexton's *Transformations*, which remixes a number of the Grimm brothers' tales.

Confession to the Moon (Sylvia Plath). Though the lines are mine, I hope that they echo a little of the subject matter and style in Plath's *Ariel* and Ted Hughes' *Birthday Letters*.

Suicide's Daughter (Sylvia Plath).

The Breast Monologues are not verbatim.

Florida (Aileen Wuornos): Sue Russell's *Lethal Intent*; Nick Broomfield's documentaries, *Aileen: Life and Death of a Serial Killer* and *Aileen Wuornos: The Selling of a Serial Killer*. The italicized statements in the poem are Wuornos's own. My friend Elizabeth is, of course, Miss Bishop.

Molly Finn (Molly Kathleen Finn). Lost at Sea, while aboard the 41 ft. sailing vessel "Free Spirit" Thursday, June 15, 2006.

Ocean State references the Rhode Island "vampire panic," which included the exhumation of Mercy Brown's body in 1892.

Teen Vamp: www.sanguinarius.org.

Hitherto Undisclosed Categories of Unfortunate Demise: The coroner's report, noted in the epigraph, was for Amy Winehouse.

Mash Up: Rush Meets Feral Pigs in the Champlain Valley is a found poem, which consists of a mishmash of lines from an article in *The New York Times* about feral pigs, "Elusive Foragers Invade Upstate New York," and Rush Limbaugh's on-air comments regarding Sandra Fluke.

Skin: Margot Mifflin's *Bodies of Subversion: A Secret History of Women and Tattoo*.

The Princess Bride (Lynda Schraufnagel). In his *Baltimore Sun* review of *The Best American Poetry* in 1992, Stephen Marguiles wrote, "Relatively unknown, Lynda Schraufnagel (who died recently at 40) gives us a trial by funkiness, a vitally weary, broken-neon-sign account of drugs and Vietnam veterans and working at diners and the guilt of refusing guilt, the numb shame of denying mercy – '… it was nothing I'd ever have to enter, nothing anyone could pin on me.'" My closest friend, she liked to call me Miss Calbert. I think it was ironic. But affectionate. As she was.

"Ophelia" (1900-1905) by Odilon Redon (1840–1916)

Previous Publishing Credits

88: "Confession to the Moon"
The Beloit Poetry Journal: "Sainted Ladies of the Middle Ages"
The Carolina Quarterly: "Nightingale"
Chelsea: "Effie Ruskin, 1849"
The Connecticut Review: "Queen Alice"
Crazyhorse: "The Wild Girl of Champagne," "Genius," "Assumption"
Green Mountains Review: "At Chawton Cottage," "Flapper," "Lizzie Borden Bed and Breakfast Museum," "Miss Bishop Has Left the Building," "Ocean State"
Hotel Amerika: "Dear Miss Dickinson," "Stunner," "Suicide's Daughter," "Talking Cure"
The Literary Review: "Fairy Tale"
Literature and Psychology: "Motherhood"
The Louisville Review: "The Princess Bride"
Michigan Quarterly Review: "'The Misses Bronte's Establishment for The Board and Education of a Limited Number of Young Ladies'"
A Narrow Fellow: "Augustine, Photographed at the Salpêtrière"
North Dakota Quarterly: "Mata Hari"
Off the Coast: "Molly Finn, Taken by the Sea"
The Paris Review: "The Lambs"
Plume: "Florida"
Poet Lore: "La Gran Ocultadora"
Pool: "Teen Vamp"
Posit: "Hitherto Undisclosed Categories of Unfortunate Demise"
Prairie Schooner: "Heretic"
The Southern Review: "Skin"

The Southwest Review: "First Wife"
TriQuarterly: "Pirating"
The Women's Review of Books: "The Afflicted Girls"

"Sainted Ladies of the Middle Ages" also appeared in *A Fine Excess: Fifty Years of the Beloit Poetry Journal.*

"Ophelia" (1889) by John William Waterhouse (1849 -1917)

Index

Poem titles are in bold and first lines in italic.

Afflicted Girls, The	10
à la mode	65
Assumption	4
At Chawton Cottage	18
At the Gonk, whiskey and White Rock	55
Augustine, Photographed at the Salpêtrière	41
"The Birth of Venus,"	65
Black rook, black pond.	60
Blood in London	52
Breast Monologues, The	67
Case of Nerves, A	28
Confession to the Moon	60
Daughter of the Revolution, you made yourself into a human piñata	56
Dear Miss Dickinson,	26
"Dora" was plagued with aphasia and vaginal catarrh	42
Eastern Venus to Duncan's Vestal Virgin	45
Effie Ruskin, 1849	33
Everyone knows	57
Everything's arranged. I have the map,	69
Fairy Tale	57
First Wife	3
First, astral bells.	35
Flapper	51

Florida	**71**
Genius	**16**
Heedlessly, Isadora let her breathtaking scarf	*64*
Heretic	**8**
Hitherto Undisclosed Categories of Unfortunate Demise	**82**
I was a boy before I became a woman.	*13*
I stuck your picture in a Kmart frame, and there you remain	*47*
I went for eleven days	*6*
I wouldn't mind sleeping with Shelley or Keats	*26*
In the morning, you can roll out	*43*
Isn't that heaven then?	*77*
It limps to my side:	*38*
Its like	*79*
Jayne Mansfield and Isadora Duncan	**64**
Jean Harlow's in Platinum Blonde	*67*
La Gran Ocultadora	**56**
Lambs, The	**20**
"Let me speak the plain truth—	24
like the Fat Lady	86
Little is known of her earthly existence	*4*
Lizzie Borden Bed and Breakfast Museum	**43**
Marriage was new for both of us.	*3*
Mash Up: Rush Meets Feral Pigs in the Champlain Valley	**84**
Mata Hari	**45**
Millais best captured your delicious passivity	*29*
Misalignment of tires or chakras	*82*
Miss Bishop Has Left the Building	**69**
"Misses Bronte's Establishment for The Board and Education	
of a Limited Number of Young Ladies, The"	**21**
Molly Finn, Taken by the Sea	**75**
Motherhood	**24**
My hair blowzy with the breeze and humidity,	*18*
New England princess, A	*62*
New Yorker	**55**

Nightingale	36
Not the immortal bird that made	36
Ocean State	77
Pirating	13
prettiest state, The	71
Princess Bride, The	87
Queen Alice	47
Rags hung from the blackened body,	12
Sainted Ladies of the Middle Ages	6
Séance	35
She donned a man's doublet and tunic,	8
Shrinks said, Inferiority complex. Yes,	51
Skin	86
smoky essence, The	52
Some said it was Unnatural	10
spider lives in my right ear, A	41
Stunner	29
Suicide's Daughter	62
sweet lady	28
Talking Cure	42
Teacher	49
Teen Vamp	79
Tucked away at Grasmere, he spooled out	16
Wandering Womb	38
We've been trading with each other:	21
Well, she is gone, mad again, and dearest Charles—	20
Who dies that kind of death these days?	75
Wild Girl of Champagne, The	12
wily elusive foragers	84
woman trapped in a statue, The	49
Yet another letter from John,	33
You took pride in being hard-hitting, unsparing,	87

ABOUT THE AUTHOR

Cathleen Calbert

The author's poetry and prose have appeared in many publications, including *Ms. Magazine, The New Republic, The New York Times,* and *The Paris Review.* She is the author of three previous books of poetry: *Lessons in Space, Bad Judgment,* and *Sleeping with a Famous Poet.* In addition to the Vernice Quebodeaux "Pathways" Poetry Prize for Women, her awards include *The Nation* Discovery Award, a Pushcart Prize, the Gordon Barber Memorial Award from the Poetry Society of America, the Sheila Motton Book Prize from the New England Poetry Club, and the Mary Tucker Thorp Award from Rhode Island College. Currently, she resides in Pacific Grove, California, with her partner and Papillons.

www.ingramcontent.com/pod-product-compliance
Lightning Source LLC
Chambersburg PA
CBHW061414090426
42742CB00023B/3461